Cross Country

Cross Country

Poems by ~~Jeff Newberry~~ and ~~Justin Evans~~

Jeff Newberry

WordTech Editions

Luke —
Thank you so much for reading this book
and supporting my and Justin's writing.
With gratitude,
Jeff

FOR Luke:
Some poems of fatherhood, art, and finding
Peace in a world in tumult. Thank you for your
support and your outlook.
Justin

Published by WordTech Editions
P.O. Box 541106
Cincinnati, OH 45254-1106

Poetry Editor: Kevin Walzer
Business Editor: Lori Jareo

Visit us on the web at www.wordtechweb.com

Acknowledgements

The authors would like to thank the editors and staff of the following publications for including poems from this book, sometimes in different forms:

Barking Sycamore Review
Clover
Communion
The Meadow
Peacock Journal
Red Rock Review
Scarlet Leaf Review
Terrain: A Journal of the Built + Natural Environments
Xavier Review

Justin would also like to thank the following people for their help and support they have given to them. Thank you: Kelli Russell Agodon, Mary Biddinger, John Gallaher, Brent Goodman, Justin Hamm, William Kloefkorn, David Lee, Jon Lee, Your support means the world.

Jeff sends gracious thanks to Ralph Adamo, Al Maginnes, Patti White, Siân Griffiths, Michael Lister, Jim Wilson, Ira Sukrungruang, and Gary McDowell. Your generosity and support mean everything to me. Jeff also thanks Heather, Ben, Madi, and the rest of The Crew. You know who you are.

A debt of gratitude is owed to Richard Hugo, whose work was the impetus for this manuscript, both in form and spirit.

Table of Contents

The Letters

1. Salutations

Letter to Evans about Words

Dear Justin—I wanted to write "Hey, man,"
or "dude" because "dear" seemed intimate,
not kiss-intimate, but intimate like sharing a couch-
intimate. Have you done that? Sat near
someone you don't know? Tried to track
conversation while you jump in
the verbal double dutch? My brother & I
used to make up curses: "ass cake" & "bastard ass"
come to mind. I used a tape deck to record
us, running through our house, screaming
a stream of obscenities. Later, listening, we
giggled at each creative swear. It was a game
you could win. Creativity mattered.
For every "dick spasm" or "fuck narding,"
I could hear my father's "dumb ass,"
his favorite words for me, the oldest son,
the one who should have been thinner,
meaner, leaner, the one who should have
been beating up neighborhood kids
& coming home with a bloodied nose,
not lying awake at night, face wet with tears,
while he pictured the earth empty,

an angry God who'd finally ruptured
the sky in rapture. When tragedy struck,
I'd dare myself to say "Damn you, God,"
or "Fuck you, God." I never even made the word
shapes on my lips. At my father's funeral,
I shared a pew with my mother & brother.
Our breaths mingled in the stale church air.
We sat too close, our fat legs touching,
suffocating each other with grief.
I wanted to say a prayer but couldn't find words.

Letter to Newberry about Words

Dear Jeff: How strange to receive
your letter this morning as I laid
in bed, the first day I felt the distance
of summer stretch out like the miles.
Take time to consider how words are
invented amongst friends. When
I was in the army, my friends and I
called each other every foul name
we could muster. It was a game,
much like yours, and when we
ran out of names, we would signal
the end of our creative outburst by
resorting to the ordinary, dull thud
of a simple "jackass" or "moron"
pretending such a name was too cruel.
Perhaps we were just being boys
as it seems you and your brother played
along similar lines, the words setting
boundaries of rivalry and superior
imaginations. There was of course
no maliciousness or harmful intent
among us, but to outsiders we must have

looked the fools to anyone uninitiated
to our fun. I, too, was the odd duck
in my family. I wandered away from
all boyhood touchstones like a lost dog—
baseball, fishing, hunting, cars. I found
pursuits but puzzled my elders and peers.
Eventually I found my own, quiet vocabulary
but that's not the same as knowing how to
speak the right words, is it?
Best, Justin

Four Attempts at a Letter about my Daughter

1.

J—
She's more than the balled knot of fear
I feel when she totters around the house

2.

I stand outside her room at night, ear to door,
& remember the NICU evenings,
when the baby in the next bed
screamed & screamed & everyone
pretended not to notice.

3.

Every step is another step
toward the day her legs may fail.
Every day, the shunt that saves
her brain may clog.
Every day is another day.

4.

If Christ can heal the broken, if Christ

can make the lame walk again,

if Christ can raise us from the stink of the grave,

if Christ can say "Forgive them,

they know not what they do,"

if Christ can—

Letter to Newberry about Past Memories of Colorado

Dear Jeff: I think we're all looking
for something, looking to run
to or from something. In my life
I have run from a lot of things—
from myself most frequently.
I paid a therapist for more than a year
to be able to say that out loud,
but I don't think it does me any
good to say it now. Maybe I will
be able to say it and mean it when
I am older, resigned to the kind of
immobility which takes a person
like a lingering winter. I waited
while my mother slowly faded away
the two years leading up to her death.
The day after she died in Grand
Junction, Colorado, I drove myself
to Elko, where I was to prepare
for a writer's workshop. To begin,
the instructor had us sit down for
what she called *sacred writing*. I

wrote how I found myself running
away from my mother, away from
my responsibilities. She had died
and I stayed distant. I could not
bring myself to call or visit her.
Your ache for distance is my regret
and I have no way to know how to
resolve either of our troubles. Your
seeming claustrophobia must itch
much the same as my desire to move
closer to the things I cannot see. If I
knew what could be done for either
of us, believe me, I would not hold
back any information. Does guilt
drive us both, like we drive along the
highways and byways of America?
Could the answer be that simple, that
we carry with us a burden we ourselves
chose to pick up as boys, before we
even could comprehend the horizons
of our future selves, let alone the past?
I look at my three boys, and I have
no idea what to tell them. Best, Justin.

Letter to Evans after a Friend Left the South

J—

A good friend moved to Colorado
& texted me the entire drive,
the oversized Penske truck
towing his wife's tiny Corolla.
He wrote *It's all silos & windmills, man.*
The closest thing I can describe
it like is the ocean, just that feeling
of size. I stand here in the claustrophobic
south, the long leaf pines & sweet gum
trees like a cage around me,
not like the open Gulf of my youth.
I ache for distance, Justin, for size.
I'm a big man, was the kind of boy
who needed Husky britches & 3X
t-shirts. I loved the ocean
because it made me feel small.
Think of a single plankton mote
dancing in the tide. It's alive
like me, but the world is built
for the thin. Ever been on a plane?
Imagine the seatbelt bifurcating

your body. Imagine the panic, the prayer
that you won't need what my brother
calls a "fat man strap," a seat belt
extender. I've been known to lean
forward & hide from the stewardess
who goes by, checking each passenger.
I know some have let me slide.
I don't order food on those flights.
I squeeze myself tight & imagine
St. Joseph's Bay, the silver-gray
water that stretched on forever.
I think of my father, a large man,
who must have lain awake,
knowing his heart was like a meter
ticking down his time here on earth.
I think of my friend Joseph,
waking to a cold Colorado dawn
& staring out at the surrounding peaks.
I think he'll think of Georgia.
I think he'll think of me.
Yours,
Another J

Letter to Newberry from the Public Library, Lexington, Nebraska

Dear Jeff: Headed towards you, finally.
Looking forward to gazing out across
the horizon in all directions, imagining
when you will be passing me in our shared
experiment in writing: You coming west to
explore and write about towns while I go east
doing much the same. When you get there,
wherever *there* might be, watch out for the rains.
Too many people believe there is no water in
the desert. This is false, and you must be careful.
Flash floods can sweep away any kindness you
may have inadvertently assigned to this part
of the world. Some places are built for the rain
but others not so much. We may not have oceans
like Florida or Georgia, but our entire world
was built by water, slowly stealing rock and dirt.
When immigrants landed in the east, they built
the world they found, when those same people
came west, they discovered a world already made;
an earth-made skyline processed by erosion—
a different sort of negative capability, carved,

polished over by time. The rocks rich in iron ore;
the blue mud in Nevada (first cast aside
while searching for gold) rich in silver; even
the pale brown rock and sand of my home, all of it
made in some way by the water which somehow
does not exist in the imaginations of those
who have not lived here. A pity. It all points to
an unfinished kingdom man has been destroying
ever since he came west. Don't get me wrong,
I think we have made objects of remarkable beauty,
but I lament how some can miss the obvious.
The emptiness of the west will soon enough
be gone, so we should not try to fill it too soon.
When you arrive, fill in that negative space
you find with all your description, be certain
to leave a little space for my imagination. I will
try to do likewise, looking for places which call out
for description, certain to leave a little wiggle room,
some small, tiny place—a corner for you to
call your own. Certainly the two of us can agree to
something as simple as that. What would you
have me beware of when I arrive in the South?
What instruction do you offer? What cautionary
advice will make my journey easier?

Yours, waiting with anticipation,

Justin

Letter to Evans on I-75 South

Dear Justin, outside Atlanta, the traffic
swells to the interstate's edge
like the tide I remember from youth,
when a hurricane threatened the coast.
You'd watch the water coming,
never a gray wall like the movies.
Think silent swelling. Think of that old story—
the frog in a boiling pot. You know
the one? Only this time, he's drowning
inch by inch until someone—let's call God
an overzealous cook—pours too much
into the pot. That's the traffic here,
man: too many frogs in one pot.
The semi trucks will force you to the shoulder
& roar on in a hot July haze.
I've imagined driving west so many times,
drinking up the miles like bourbon,
& enjoying the hazy drunk that follows.
I imagine life thinning—the grass winnowing,
losing one, two, three trees every thirty
miles, buildings retreating into the earth,
until all that's left is a sepia landscape

of desert and stone. I find solace
in silence, Justin. I like the way
my ears ring after a while, songs
that play constantly in my mind.
My friend the Buddhist tells me
happiness is avoiding suffering.
I think happiness is silence—
but that vacuum scares me.
The traffic here never stops, despite
the good ole boys who like to believe
we all live in some rural paradise.
A friend from Idaho told me when she arrived
in Georgia, everything seemed crowded,
closed in. Nothing is more than a twenty-minute
drive away. In Moscow, she said, the mountains
shelter valleys no one's darkened for twenty years.
That's the place I want to be if only
so I can imagine what it must be like here,
the place I've left behind.

Letter to Newberry: June 14, 2016

Dear Jeff: Woke up to another shooting,
this one in Florida. Received your letter
earlier this evening. Of course we
have no answers, only clichés that have
lost all meaning. I 'played army' as a child,
grew up with guns, served in the army,
learned how to throw grenades, becoming
the envy of some childhood friends when
I went to war. Funny how none of them
paid much attention when I told them
stories of serving graves registration, going
out to various locations to retrieve bodies—
three Iraqi soldiers, one missing a hand,
another with his skull crushed by a tank.
Stranger still was their silence when I tried
telling them how amnesty boxes were put
in place because American soldiers had
been taking human ears, fingers, and arms
as trophies—the result of too many
shitty movies about the Vietnam war.
It's why I never bought into the bullshit
of thanking vets my age or younger for

their service. I served with a lot of good men
but I also know the capacity for human
stupidity. Sometimes I think I try to use
too many words to express my anger; where
I see other poets excise, I become verbose,
try to purge myself of all language, expel
every ounce of emotion. I fear the day
will come when I will need my words but
there will be nothing left. I will be empty,
unable to conjure even the disappointment
of a platitude that has soured like milk,
leaving a void to be filled by fear, or worse,
by bullets. Soon enough we will not be singing
a requiem for the lost, but one for ourselves.
Soon enough, there will be no one left to sing.
Yours in peace, Justin

Letter to Evans after Orlando, after Sandy Hook

I've never owned a real gun—never
wanted one. As a child, I idolized soldiers & killing,
thrived on Vietnam War movies
& thought John Rambo a national treasure.
My friends bought Dollar Store AK-47s
& stalked the jungles of our backyard imaginations.
We dodged invisible grenades & killed
"gooks" and "wops" because we wanted to show
each other our manliness. I was a fat kid, Justin—
my boy boobs jiggled behind an ill-fitted
K-Mart camouflage t-shirt. My breath wheezed
through lungs made shallow by nights
of Little Debbie cakes & RC Cola. I had to prove
to them I could run, had to show them nothing
scared me. My narratives were the bloodiest,
the violent tales of bouncing betties taking a man's legs
out in a red haze. I slaughtered scores to prove I loved
America, to make them love me even more. I never
served, Justin, to answer a friend's question,
who interrogated me in the days after Iraq,
when I wondered why we'd waded into yet
another quagmire. My father did his four years

& ditched the Air Force after the Cuban Missile Crisis.
He told me he lay in his bunk & waited for the world
to end. Tonight, I'm listening to my son run
through the house, telling his cousin, "I'm gonna kill you"
because the boy had taken my son's toy. I laugh
& know that it's not serious. He's only got
a water pistol. His rights are safe.
He can walk into a night club or high school
tomorrow, free as an ejected shell.

2. Credo

Letter to Evans: Like Waves Breaking

> *It's a cold and it's a broken Hallelujah.*
> —Leonard Cohen

> *What if God kept a secret?*
> —Mark Jarman

i.

Dear Justin, I just watched my daughter
vomit up a dinner of hot dogs & graham crackers.
Standard toddler stuff—congestion & mucus
have clogged her system for three days now.
The story I write is different: Spina Bifida.
She was born with a hole in the base of her spine.
An internal tube drains fluid from her brain
to her abdomen. A clogged shunt can kill,
cause brain damage. One sign of a shunt
malfunction? Vomiting. Every childhood
scar or stumble leads me back to her disease,
my unease knowing her this way—not
a child, a disorder, not my daughter,
a future in a wheelchair, should her legs
one day seize. A one-day-this-could-happen.
A vision of bowel management enemas,

of self-cathing. Not of school plays.
Not of girl slumber parties, whispered secrets
around a backyard fire. Not of dance camps
or track meets or dances or homecoming queen.
It all mutates into one phrase: Spina Bifida.
I'm trying to push the dreams into place,
the way you might shape biscuit dough,
knowing that if you handle it too much,
the butter will melt & the biscuits won't rise.
Listening to her breathe on a monitor,
I take each breath with her, willing my lungs
do the work for her. She sleeps & I sleep.
Tomorrow, we will do this all again.

ii.

They said my son would be deformed.

They said he was too big for my wife's womb.

They told my wife they had to induce her.

That night, after sixteen hours of labor

& an emergency c-section, he came

into the world, a screaming mass of flesh.

He was undersized & I laughed

at worried doctors who saw my girth

& assumed a colossus of a fetus.

His eyes were blue like marbles.

I didn't know all baby's eyes are blue.

I thought he'd always have eyes like a cat.

Later, the color became river water.

It's too easy to say he's just like me,

too easy to say he's a better version.

He's child of God, just like you or me.

The Bible teaches me we're born under a curse.

To breathe, it seems, is sin. He stumbles

through life, my clumsy boy, nine-years-old,

silly in the way boy children are. He laughs

at everything from internet fodder

to his friends' drawings of oversized faces.

I gave him a child-sized guitar when he

turned four. He swung it like a battle-axe

& it broke, denting the sheetrock in his room.

He tried piano & it didn't take. His voice,

though, sounds like a sparrow at dawn,

high-pitched as though fluted through glass.

It weaves around melodies, finds harmonies,

never flattens or sharpens outside his will.

He sings like his mother, with the ease

you or I have with words. That's a lie,

right? Our voices on the page come

from silent muses who communicate

when we're not listening, who urge us

with hand gestures and mute head nods.

Maybe that's the real talent. It comes despite

the rough work. I've spent half my life

scribbling words to make the world

make sense. The night he was born,

they wrapped my son in a blanket

& put him in my arms. Finally, I thought,

someone who will mourn me

when I'm gone. Finally, someone

who will know how to sing my song.

iii.

In a graveyard in Southwest Georgia,
a four-by-two headstone reads
"Laura Suzanne Newberry"
with a single date: December 28, 1982.
Beneath the date: *A little bud of love*
to bloom with God above. I never knew
my sister. A tangled umbilical cord wrapped
her neck in utero, dooming her birth,
killing her the day she emerged in our broken
world. My father alone made the journey
from North Florida for her funeral.
The rest coalesced in our rented home,
huddled near a gas space heater
my mother swore would one day blow
us all to kingdom come. My father told
me a few year later that months
after her death, he walked along the shore
of Cape San Blas, angry with God,
& had a vision of—something. I don't
know. He didn't say. He couldn't say.
I just knew that I'd heard & seen God
he told me. Eight years later,

his heart gave out, clogged from decades
of cigarettes & nightly twelve-packs.
There is no other way to say this:
he was not a good father. He hit
my mother, hit his boys. I used to blame
him for Laura's death. God had used her
to show him the spring ice fragility
of life. Then I blamed God. I spit venom
at Him for years. I used to lie
awake in college & dare Him to face me,
to explain Himself to me, to make His
will perfectly clear, if only once.
My sister had red hair, my mother says,
long red hair. I can picture it when I try.
When I close my eyes, though, the first
image is the tombstone, cold & silent.

iv.

I worry about blood pressure, worry about weight.
I think about the growing uric acid in my blood,
the pain in my feet & knees. I picture a brown-black
coffin where some undertaker will lay me
& shave me one last time. He'll fold my hands
over my spent heart. My wife will tell him
I look *natural* & *good*. I've never wanted
to be buried. For years, I've said I want cremation.
I want my ashes scattered in the Gulf of Mexico,
to return to the salt waters from which I emerged.
Our bodies are water, Justin, but not living water.
You can't drink salt water. The earth is 70% water,
too, & the tide's rising as we abuse our world.
You can't drink most of that water. Imagine dying
of thirst on a ship in a silent Sargasso.
Imagine looking out at the acres of blue,
the clusters of clouds, & going mad, taking draughts
from cupped palms, knowing that the salt will
suck your insides dry, that even as your parched
lips burn, you're dying. Christ called himself
"Living Water," said we his people were to be
"Salt and Light," & I've got half of that right.

I dream of a ship sailing toward the east,

laden with spices & cargo, me at the stern,

finding my way home one more time.

Leonard Cohen sang that Jesus was a sailor

when he walked upon the ocean.

I've spent many years in my own lonely wooden

tower. I've sang broken chords in broken words.

I cling to splintered driftwood in a hurricane,

feeling the water swirl around me,

waiting on the tide to take me down.

I remain your faithful friend,

Jeff

Letter to Newberry: Personal History

It is not flesh and blood but the heart
which makes us fathers and sons.
—Schiller

Dear Jeff: It all comes down to fathers
& sons, right? All our clamoring, worries,
our scribbles — issues which haunt us
in our dreams night like prophesy. Chasing
all our lives a father of some kind,
fearing our inadequacies will be the thing
to shape our children instead of intentions.
I don't know my own father, the man whose
seed formed me in my mother's womb. Shortly
after my mother died, my older sister revealed
the family secret which everyone was able to
keep from me for forty years. My mother took
to heart the spirit of the free love counterculture
taking to lovers like long hair takes to the wind.
The man who is my father was just another
distraction from her husband, the man who
accepted me as his own, even if only *pro-forma*,
for the sake of appearances. I was born cesarean;
my mother's narrow hips required it of

43

all four of her births, making me wonder
if I would be here had I been conceived after
Roe v. Wade, being her only conception
born of a man she did not actually love. It is
one of the questions I will never be able
to ask. It was my mother's wish I be kept
ignorant of these things until after she died
so on some level I know she cared enough
to spare me the doubts my circumstances
carry. When I teach *Hamlet* in school
I do not explain how my own experiences
enlarge my thoughts of the play, how I
have questioned the basis of my own
existence on more than an academic level;
how when I asked my father about these things
he admitted the truth, stopping short of
explaining why he fought for custody
or placed me with his parents when I became
too much to ask of his second wife. Actions
which I cannot deny saved my life.
I mean that, too, my friend. I cannot say
where I would be if he had left me with
my mother and her transient life,
moving from one man to the next.

*

After my parents divorced, she lived with
one of her many affairs, a man, who
returned from the military after being
wounded in Vietnam. All appearances
say they loved each other, addiction likely
the basis, for their affections.
My mother's third child, a son, born
the day after this man died in jail.
He had been arrested writing bad checks.
1973 Utah was still a conservative world
& the county coroner listed his death
from unknown causes— a mother's blessing
who would not hear of the truth
of addiction. This man had been
a surrogate father for me, and though he
had been discharged a private
under less than honorable conditions for
drugs (a common problem of the time)
I knew nothing of that, & I called him
My captain, a foreshadowing perhaps
of things to come in later years. After
his death, likely caused by my mother
smuggling drugs into the jail. His father, a

strong man who raised horses, showed me
kindness as his son had. Some twenty years
later, on leave from the same army
which certainly turned his son to drugs,
I visited this man as he lay dying, a stroke
having stolen his speech. We sat in silence
for a long time. My last image of him was
his crying, using his last ounce of energy
to give voice to what he wanted to say.
As the years linger, pull me closer to
resembling this man lying in the bed,
& farther away from the young man
I was while watching him struggle
I understand grief even more.

*

Living with the man I thought was my father
didn't last. My sister could provoke me
& I could not stop. When I was seven
he asked his parents to take me, raise me,
give me the home I needed. They agreed,
taking me in with conditions, one being
my itinerant life would end. There would be
no back and forth, recall, or reckoning. I was
their son. That was that. Some years later
my grandfather asked to adopt me, but
my father said, *No*. I have no idea for
his reasons, no way to know what
stopped him from agreeing. My father
with his second wife & kids lived fifteen
minutes away, visited frequently. When they
arrived I would hopelessly seek his affection
to no avail. He cut ties which forty years
later puzzles me like a magician's trick.
Perhaps his doubts were verified, my looks—
half my mother's, half not his—too much
a daily reminder. Whatever his cause, it was
that singular choice which saved me from
my mother's cult of loss, having surrendered

47

her third child to his aunt (a reunion
which took forty years to carve from
the granite quarry of time). While I had
my father's father, my brother searched in vain,
picked up where his father left, finding
drugs and theft like a pig rooting for truffles.

*

I was lucky. I admit that. I have spent my life
looking, collecting fathers, grandfathers,
scoutmasters, Sunday school teachers, soldiers,
& professors—each one incomplete, but each
giving me another piece. Zen writings explain
how the journey is more than the destination,
how searching itself can be the instruction
we seek. I do not know my own mind when
thinking of my pursuit. After five decades
I still don't know if it is a father I seek
or the idea of a father. As a father myself, I
understand what you are saying, though
I cannot know the specifics of your fears.
I think being a father eludes all men, like chasing
a flock of birds or school of fish, their sudden
orchestrated shifts from necessity but graceful
& beautiful at a distance. For all my searching
I have fewer answers than I had when I first
began my journey, setting out like Telemachus
with nothing more than the wind and a sail.
My three sons are not a tv sit-com; I have
made mistakes which reject twenty-three
minute-three commercial resolutions. I imagine

myself at the end of my life, trying in vain to
pass on what I know as I ignore all my fears
about finite existence. Therein lies my secret—
I will sacrifice my sons at the altar of manhood
while chasing after a father who has never
truly existed for me, and a commandment
I will never fully comprehend.
Sincerely,
Justin

3. Chosen

Letter to Evans about the Doctrine of Preordination

Imagine the terrible weight of having God
on your side. You must walk assured
that each vow you break, each bug you kill,
each face you scar with the face you've prepared—
all is preordained, sanctioned. My friend
the pastor tells me that I'm wrong, that God
doesn't use us like puppets. He preaches
three-point sermons footnoted with Luther
& Calvin. He thinks guns and God
are one in the same, thinks only sheep trust
the government, sees me as misguided,
a fool not to answer with folly. I think
of a guy we used to call "Preacher Man"
when I was a kid. He rode around
on a three-wheeled trike & told all who'd listen
that the Kingdom was at hand. He said
my brother's best friend Ben couldn't go
to heaven because Ben is black & animals
don't go to heaven. He quoted an obscure
Old Testament verse meant to show heaven
a white-washed Caucasian paradise. Preacher Man

handed out Chick tracts & I'll confess, some nights
I lay in bed and shuddered, imagining literal fire
& brimstone, wondering if I were an enemy
of the Most High. The angel touched
Isaiah's lips to burning coal & told the prophet
his guilt had been taken away. I bite myself
daily & probe the wounds with my tongue.
I've been doing that since I was a kid.
You'd think I would have learned by now.

Letter to Newberry: Shadenfreude

And I looked, and behold a pale horse: and his name that sat on him was
Death, and Hell followed with him. And power was given unto them over
the fourth part of the earth, to kill with sword, and with hunger, and with
death, and with the beasts of the earth.
—Revelation 6:8

When I hear the word culture *I reach for my pistol*
—Hanns Johst (often misattributed to Hermann Göring)

Dear Jeff:

Leave it to the Germans to manufacture

a word to suit every mood or feeling

no matter how obscure or specialized.

After these last few news cycles I could

have sworn it finally was the apocalypse

I saw outside my window— all the signs

were there; all the desolation, Hell following

fast on the heels of the Anti-Christ, both

Clinton and Trump being decried as the one

and each also being upheld as America's

savior. Can there be any hope left that

both might retreat back to whence they came,

back to a time before they were all we

could think or talk about? Just one month

remains, but I want to be finished with it all;

I want to strike a box of matches, set fire
to this world, give the physical manifestation
of fire to a world already on fire. There is
no subtle way to put it. We have devolved
to the point where the two most hated people
in our nation are asking for our love and
an almost unfettered power. I am almost
ashamed to admit I no longer care who wins
because Thomas Jefferson was right: *We
always get the rulers we deserve*, and for the
first time in many years we all will be forced
to share in the shame of electing the end
result of finding joy in the suffering of others.
I have heard some call for the return to
Civility and others demanding to return
America to some imagined greatness, and all
I can think to say is each is merely different
sides of the same coin, and I want to play
Annie Oakley and Buffalo Bill, tossing
that coin into the air for a quick-draw shot.

Letter from St. Augustine, the Oldest City

star (noun): a fixed luminous point in the night sky that is a large, remote incandescent body like the sun

I Jesus have sent mine angel to testify unto you these things in the churches. I am the root and the offspring of David, and the bright and morning star.
—Revelation 22:16

My cross-country friend: when I was a child,
I used to lie down in the back
of my parent's station wagon
when we drove home at night
& stare at the domed bowl of sky.
On moonless nights, the spotlights
at Tyndall Air Force Base near my home
shone sharp blades of light
& I wondered where they ended.
Light never ends. I would one day.
One day, no one will ever know
I was even here. At ten, the openness
of space turned my stomach.
I felt tiny, insignificant, just a voice
whispering with awe into a canyon.
My voice never bounced back
because I stayed silent.

Tears streaked down my cheeks
for reasons I still don't grasp.
Here in America's Oldest City™
you can visit the Fountain of Youth.
It's just swamp, nothing special,
not a tide pool that will roll back
years the way some say Christ
will roll back the heavens one day.
I imagine Ponce de Leon, half-mad
with bug bites, slashing his way
though the Florida wilderness.
How the forest would have hummed.
The sky was an unscarred blue blade.
How angry he must have been,
rising, the waters still streaming
down his face, still the same age
he'd been. I know he imagined
some moment in his childhood,
when he stared up at the sky,
saw the burned embers of stars
& felt the pull of immortality.

Letter to Newberry from Lake of Fire Valley, Sunrise

Dear Jeff: Woke up early to watch the sunrise
slowly appear over the Bonneville Salt Flats,
where the horizon curves, like Diana's bow.
As expected, the birds began singing before
the sun's corona was much more than a hint—
a cacophony of doves and barn swallows
which I try to ignore most mornings, but can
forgive today as I watch the sky begin to
transform into its bright countenance. I have
seen morning thousands of times here, in this
desert. This place has been my home longer
than any other place. For seventeen years
I have lived and worked amid the sagebrush;
stretched out from my relative isolation to the
world at large while my sons have grown
themselves and started searching for their own
identities. The majority of what I know about
poetry and my meager successes have come
while I look out into this same valley, marking
each small variation of morning or evening
into the recesses of an ever shifting memory—

all with the hope it will serve me when I call.
I cannot say the years have come and gone
with ease, or swift as an arrow or barn swallow,
but I can declare time has had its way with me
fusing the years into a single, gradual tapestry
much like how the sky changes starry black
to pale blue and back into itself, all without
a single declaration of change. I owe myself
to this place—everything I am in one way
or another—a most Hegelian synthesis. With
each passing breath I am becoming more a part
of this lonely valley, and with each exhale
I am sending word to the world, anyone who
would listen, what it is to let one's self unite
with the earth without a pre-requisite death.
All the best, Justin

Letter to Evans: Brexit

The news is division—broken borders,
forgotten alliances. The news is old
people vs. young people. The news
is conservative vs. progressive,
Democrat vs. Republican, white vs. brown,
earth vs. sky, fact vs. fiction.
Think of the truth as A union B.
I have been lost in the Venn diagram
since I was a child. My friend
the extremist sees Brexit as a "sign
of things to come." He claims patriotism
but wants our country broken.
He posts about secession on Twitter
& arm chairs the evening news.
He calls me a "statist" & thinks I worship
at D.C.'s altar. My father confessed
communism to me one night
as we worked a paper route we shared.
At fourteen, I was a Hollywood patriot,
raised on Rambo & *The A-Team*.
He said *I don't see why we can't all*
have one big pile of money & share it.

Years later, I think of him, a broken
man, divided against himself—
backwards-looking, pining for years gone
but progressive enough to think the world
a fixable place. He was an artist
who never found an audience,
a songwriter, a cartoonist, a creator
imprisoned by Reagan's trickle-down voodoo.
My extremist friend would have hated
my father, would have called him evil.
Whitman wrote "vivas for those who have failed."
I celebrate myself for all of my failures.
My father and my friend and me—
every atom belonging to each of us is shared.
There is no schism here. We can't
vote away our connection.

Letter to Newberry: Brexit, Texit, and the New American Migration

Dear Jeff: I say let them all go—
Texas, the Tea Party, the cult
of Donald Trump. Let them all go.
It's not polite, but we both know
what part of the past they yearn for,
which *past* they think separates us
from half a century of godlessness.
We all have friends who call this
a Christian Nation in one breath
then shout at the tops of their lungs
how we are losing our religion in
the next. We all know some version
of the Texas mother who shot her
two daughters dead in the street
ever fearful of Obama coming
to take away her guns. I am not
saying we don't know honorable
conservatives, but it seems their
voices have been lost, swallowed
by the anger of a white America
gullible enough to believe one

black President is enough to sound
the death knell to the American
experiment. It's generational, like
anti-vaccine advocates. You won't
hear your grandparents talking about
the dangers of inoculations, nor
anyone who saw first hand the
ravages of Polio or Diphtheria.
Most of the people who hold Reagan
up as a Neo-Con Messiah never
went more than a day without food
or saw desperation in their parents.
Sometimes you have to separate
the wheat from the chaff, let the wind,
winnow the husk from the harvest.
Walt Whitman asked if the elder races
had stopped, ended their lessons.
I add to this my own resolute question:
At what point do we stop marching
forward? If they are not interested
in taking the next step, then perhaps
we should let them leave, saving us
the burden they are and the limits
of their myopia. All the best, Justin.

4. Helicon

Letter to Evans: I was a Preteen Werewolf

In fourth grade, I told
my friend Jamie that I was a werewolf.
I told him I arose on full-moon
nights & stalked our small towns,
eating stray dogs & cats,
the occasional deer who'd wandered
too far from the underbrush.
I said I awoke some mornings
in my backyard, wet with dew,
the blood of last night's kill
still staining my t-shirt & shorts.
Then, I'd pull back my lips
& show my canine teeth,
which angled out in pointed shards.
I didn't tell him the insides
of my lips were stippled
with scar tissue. I never
said when I bit myself eating,
blood poured from my mouth,
& the wound pulsed for hours,
a hole I'd probe with a bored tongue
during class or after school,

when my brother & I came home
to an empty house, my father
still at the paper mill, my mother
working a split shift. We'd watch
Andy Griffith on a black & white TV
& imagine our dad like Andy,
a man too good to carry a gun.
Our father drank himself into a coma
each night. Red & white cans of Budweiser
overflowed the kitchen garbage,
& he'd sometimes strike my mother
in rage, this gentle artist I'd seen
write songs & draw cartoons,
this man who became a monster.
No dentist ever saw my teeth.
Years later, in my twenties, I visited
one who told me I should have
been fitted for braces as a child.
I didn't tell him that my parents
were too poor to ever take me.
I didn't tell him that I'd once
been a werewolf. I just said
"Yeah, you're probably right,"
& ran my tongue over my scars
& tasted all the years built up there.

Letter to Newberry Considering the Moon

Someone has spilled the moon
all over the trees;
—Linda Pastan

Dear Jeff: When I see the moon shift
on a daily basis on my walk to school,
days seemingly fade ever on into the past—
I try to think of how many different
variations each of us have, how many
gifts we might possess worthy of
offer, worthy of what and who we are
in relation to the world around us.
The moon walks through eight phases, as its
pale circumference follows the earth
like a heartbroken child. Often times
I wonder where it would go if it wasn't
tethered to us for all eternity, or why it
sticks around if it has given all it can or
all it wants. I want to know what is
so special about us that we are blessed
with such inordinate beauty. We can say
we are simply favored by God, or
blessed with tremendous, cosmic luck,

but I do not want a simple answer
tonight. I want to see the mystery unfold,
complex as it might be. I want to see a
re-creation of the Creation. I want to see
firsthand what the moon was given
to give us— what the moon carries inside
like an egg. Sometimes I want to break
open the moon and cause its treasure to
spill all over the fertile earth, just to watch
what might grow, eventually leaping
into outer space to fill the void.
All the best, Justin.

Letter to Evans from Decatur: Eliot, Jazz, & Peace

I'm sitting in a Decatur, Georgia,
motel room & thinking of Michael Harper,
who wrote he had a friend
who'd risen above jazz.
I tell him to stay there, the poem
says. I feel the same way
about politics: I want to rise
above it & stay there.
I'm not the enlightened speaker
of the poem this time, heavy
with epiphany & sacred knowledge.
I've taken to signing some emails
"Shantih," that peace that surpasseth all,
& I wonder who among
my recipients bothers Googling
the term, & I feel the weight of guilt
by assuming they don't know the word.
Robert Pinsky said he knew a pipe fitter
who read poetry. I once worked
for an IGA grocery store & the milkman
was the spitting image of Phil Levine,

bad teeth & all. I couldn't tell
him "Shantih." We smoked cigarettes
in silence before unloading
gallons of Borden milk,
the jugs sweaty, wet in the morning
humidity. I remember their fat weight
in my hands, how I groaned
each time I lifted a crate of four,
how that exhaled breath was a kind
of poem. The milkman said
that black people wanted to take over
the world. Back then, that scared me—
anyone taking over the world scared me—
now, I'd say, "White folks haven't done
such a good job running the place.
Let them have it." Shantih shantih shantih.

Letter to Newberry about my Visit to Angel Lake, Nevada

Dear Jeff: Drove up to Angel Lake
nestled high above the small town of
Wells, Nevada. It's the type of place
you might expect to find in Europe,
a small alpine lake, most might
consider nothing more than a pond,
but more than adequate for helping to
excise the demons of my mind—
Politici americanus. The clean air
at 8,400 feet is free from pollution
and more important, the vitriol of
this election cycle which started far
too soon. The only sounds heard:
birds, insects, water, and leaping fish,
are more than enough to blot out
the anger of uninformed arguments
shouted from the left and the right.
While filling out my parking permit
I saw an external hearing aid mic left
on top of the fee box—a perfect
metaphor for this lake—someone

leaving behind the world to enter
a different world where one might
hear with their own ears, unfettered
by external apparatus or translation.
Looking back from the lake, I could
see the vast serenity of Clover Valley
spreading out like a floral quilt,
muffling the tumult of commentary.
Of course that hearing aid was waiting
for their owner's return and decent
back into the place where we all live
but for a brief moment they were free
from constrain and extremism; able
to breathe easier. Have you ever heard
the words, 'Altitude, not Attitude'
in your years of reading? Having been
to this small mountain lake I can say
with some certainty, they are true.
Do you have some distant place,
far from the rest of the word, a retreat
where you can shut out the world?
I plan to return to Angel Lake, where

I hope to find the sound of my own heart.

All the best, Justin

Letter to Evans in a Year Without a Winter

I keep waiting for the cold to arrive,
keep thinking it's stalled somewhere,
maybe out on I-75, pulled to the side
of the road, hood up. The block burps
oil-black smoke. I keep thinking
about my father, who said it never got
as cold as it did when he was a kid,
or as hot either. I keep thinking
Entropy & how the world will slow
one day, how the real order of the universe
seems an urge to rest. Past forty now,
I think of death all the time: heart
disease, cancer, cardiac arrest,
a list culled from what once seemed
old man diseases. A bleary head
after a bad night's sleep is a tumor's
seed, black tentacles nascent in my skull.
I imagine my funeral far too often.
A friend has a playlist long as a double album
& urges me to *Drink up* at his send-off.
I keep thinking I'm slowing down,
& I'm not sure if I am. I keep thinking

I've broken down on this journey to my life.
Somewhere, someone's waiting on me.
Someone checks the door from time to time,
scans the road for my car. Someone
settles in a chair in an empty room
& drums bony fingers, marking time.

Letter to Newberry while listening to Mozart's 9th Piano Concerto

And Elijah said unto Ahab, Get thee up, eat and drink; for there is a sound of abundance of rain.
—1 Kings 18:41

Thou, O God, didst send a plentiful rain, whereby thou didst confirm thine inheritance, when it was weary.
—Psalms 68:9

Dear Jeff: This morning the Nevada skies
are filled with gray clouds and threaten
a mild rain, unlike the torrents of water which
fell upon us weeks ago, where every corner of
this town was submerged. A rare occurrence—
one I have never seen before in my eighteen
years living in these northern alkali deserts.
The small taps of rain which might fall today
will not threaten anything, nor will they
bury this place in their fury. Their small dance
will merely foreshadow winter storms
most certain to pass overhead in the coming
months. It is not the season for growth, but
rain for us is never a constant, so in these times of
drought we will take whatever falls and be
happy for it. After winter passes and the desert

turns its thoughts to spring, the cactus will bloom
and sagebrush will paint the valley green. Tomorrow
the red rock and sandstone formations etched
by ancient Bonneville will look freshly painted;
sunrise will present a broad corona of pale blue
light—perhaps the year's last before mornings
begin to bite the ears and fingers of children
walking to school. Today's rain, if any comes, will
be a concerto in the classical sense, three brief
movements to accentuate the day's journey,
usher us from one end to the other in a seamless
fashion, beginning with an Allegro of cloud and wind
transitioning into an Andantino, where
the scent of rain is thick, ending then with a Rondeau Presto
of tiny drops—nothing serious or taxing.
The Lord giveth us the rain, maketh the heavens
to open up when we are righteous as to know
His love and wish that we firmly know abundance
in harvest. In this knowledge we may see the world
turn as it must, as it was originally composed.

All the best,
Justin.

Letter to Evans about Hurricanes

Dear Justin—

In 95, Opal took our home, just three years after my father
breathed his last lying in a hospital bed. How my mother
didn't kneel in rage & scream at the universe, I do not know.
I don't know how she saw the hole in the side of that bayside
home, looked at me & my brother, big, bulky boys,
& said *We'll be okay.* In '82, she lost the baby, a sister I mourn
sometimes the way you might an ancestor you never met.
Laura Suzanne they called her. The umbilical cord tied round
her neck in the womb. How my mother didn't find fault
in herself I don't know—maybe she did. Maybe she lies
awake some nights & wishes for ghosts, tangible & real.
I still drive by the place our house once stood, that rented
shack. Y-weeds & tangled grass in sand. The palm tree gone.
The slash pines gone. Once I dreamed Death drove
a hurricane the way you or I might drive a car, dropped
into gear as he headed toward the coast, revving the engine.
He wanted to cause as much damage as possible.
There's no place to stand after a storm's wiped a town away.

You stare & gape at ghosts of buildings & wonder
they were ever real at all. Without the signs,
do streets have names? If you can't recall them, no.

~Jeff

Letter to Newberry Regarding Rituals

Dear Jeff: The other day I was boiling
pine nuts I bought at a roadside stand,
the scent filling the house, my tongue
anticipating the familiar taste I knew as a boy
when my grandfather would harvest cones
every year, tend them like coffee beans. He
knocked them out of the tree, carried them home
to rake them over the course of several weeks
as they dried, opened up enough to be shucked
two seeds at a time from each scale. After,
he would sort out the bad nuts while washing
them, bag the good, hang them from our
garage walls. Some years he would harvest
more than a hundred pounds, giving away
bags to family and friends, rather than selling
them. My grandfather could have made a profit,
but chose to go the other way. One neighbor
was an amateur meteorologist, who kept records
of everything— he would ask my grandfather
whether his harvest was bountiful or lean; a way
to predict the following winter, he believed.
For years my grandfather roasted the nuts, then
he switched to boiling them in salt water,

their shells softening, taking on the slightest
suggestion of flavor. I remember so much
about him, but this is one of my favorite
memories, perhaps because the simple ritual
of gathering pine nuts lasted in one way or another
most of the year, and I knew from the way
he busied himself with them was the same as he
approached any job, with fastidious care.
My grandfather has since passed on, more than
a decade ago, but smell being the strongest
trigger for memory, I can always conjure him
from the past, bring him up to the forefront
of my mind, replay this complex ritual as if
the barrier between life and death did not exist.
All the best, Justin.

Letter to Evans from a Montgomery, Alabama, Motel Room

I fell in love with language when my father
sang "Hound Dog" and banged out four chords
on a no-name guitar. Something rose
in my spirit like death, a spirit in my chest—
& I knew I had to get a fix again,
so I raided his records & played Sam Cooke,
felt that sad mood move through me like wine.
I scoured bargain bins for cast-off
tunes. I laughed at Pizza Hutt after church youth
group one night when a girl asked me
What kind of music do you like?
I said *Roy Orbison is my favorite singer.*
She said *He's kind of old, isn't he?* This was '85.
If I could go back down, I'd show her my calloused
fingertips & say *The mood never gets old.*
Only the lonely understand. When my father died,
I made a god of song & poems & tried to reforge
a shattered life. I followed syllables where they took
me. I sat in a sophomore literature survey
& felt my spirit skip when Eliot's "Prufrock"
scratched a groove in my soul. Later, still,

Richard Hugo showed me the beauty in a place
no one wanted to see. I've been to Philipsburg,
go there often. I buy tickets from my reflection
& sit in a train car all alone. Now, here
in this southern city, I wonder what my father
would say about my books, my words, the stories
I've woven together like used-up guitar strings.
I like to think he'd shake his head. I like to think
he'd want me to pick up a guitar & teach him
a new tune. I like to think he'd still be
hustling for that long lonesome song.

Letter to Newberry After my Son's Honorable Discharge

—Hebrews 4:12

Dear Jeff: In basic training we were taught
there are only two kinds on the battlefield:
the quick and the dead. Or, at least
that's the way I remember it in all my
cinematic dreams—the two edged sword of God
coming down from the heavens, burning
with the heat of a 155mm Howitzer round
which has an uncanny talent for separating
bone from ligature and flesh from sinew.
Two weeks ago my son returned from
four years in the navy, four years of boredom
with nothing dangerous, and nothing to
write home about. I welcomed him, thankful
we did not have the experience of combat
to share in silence the rest of our lives. I
pretend sometimes I never was in the army
trying to imagine how my life would differ,
how I might see things through different lenses
never knowing the half-weight of a dead man,
the smell of a blood stained leather bound Quran.

Gone are the days I would kneel and pray
God enter my heart to heal the scars of war—
With each passing day I might know more
about myself, but I know less about the hearts
of my fellow man. If I were to pray for anything
I would probably ask that I be allowed to
forget the cadence and rituals of my war
relearning who I was before I knew how to
empathize with the quick and the dead.

Letter to Evans: On Writing the Dead

Dear Justin—the ghost I saw
in the hallway when I was
ten may have been a trick
of the light. Perhaps shadows
shifted as the pines groaned
in the wind. Maybe I made
a face of silhouette & porch light—
pareidolia. I've always spoken
to the dead & felt them near.
I've never seen them, not even
felt them. Still, I see my father's
face each morning when I shave.
My heart races from time to time
& I imagine a sick hospital
stench, where he lay wrapped
in green sheets as his heart expired.
I think of my grandfather's
palsied hand in those last
moments, the .22 rifle barrel
nestled on his tongue.
The steel tastes cold & final.
I used to pray for midnight

visions, dreams of the dead.
My father's never spoken to me
from beyond. I've yearned
for just a hint—a whiff
of his aftershave, the acrid
stench of a cigarette, my name
whispered when no one's around.
I write them to life—my father
& grandfather. I study them
on white paper, lines of words
that, if I tilt my head just so,
if I squint my eyes just right,
make a mask, a face, a me.

Letter to Newberry: The Dead Write Back

The dead know only one thing, it is better to be alive
—*Stanley Kubrick,* Full Metal Jacket

Dear Jeff: I am very sorry
the dead have not taken time
to speak to you all these years
you have known them. I have
heard from the dead many times,
been privy to their whispers
disguised as bare branches
scraping against a window, or
rubbing against vinyl siding.
Believe me when I tell you
it isn't nearly as eventful as one
might think. The Dead seem
only to know one thing, and
continually lament again and
again like the rippling water
of a small creek or the clacking
of a train passing through town.
In fact, I gave up listening
many years ago, after learning

for myself they cannot give us
the answers we need; and we
will never be able to give them
what they want. I do not know the
pain you are feeling, the sense of
something vital being stopped
prematurely, taken from you,
being cut loose from the earth
with nothing to tether you to
the eternal spirit of ancestry.
The only comfort I can give you
is to say your writing is not a
vanity or waste of time. Each
word you write is salve, each
line you create is a hymn waiting
to be picked up by the dead
in hopes they can someday learn
how to at last speak to you.

5. P.S.

Letter to Evans: The Year without Summer

Dear Justin—the year she wrote Frankenstein,
Mary Shelley lived in a year without summer.

Mount Tambora exploded the previous spring,
spewing ash into our climate cycles, blocking

the sun. Crops failed. They say peasants wandered
the English roads by the thousands, refugees

seeking asylum in cities. Food shortages.
Doomsday cults. A muddy, frost-sludged year

of rain. How appropriate that the young Mary
imagined not a better world but an intensification

of her own: a sutured creature shocked to life
& hunted by its creator. This is no reimagined

Genesis, no creation myth for a new year.
This is the story of humanity, forever stalking

itself to recover itself, to understand itself.

In my mind, I don't see Karloff. I see myself.

Letter to Newberry: For the Year 2016

Farewell remorse!
All good to me is lost;
Evil, be thou my Good
—Milton

Dear Jeff: We all have our own wasteland,

the realization we are both master and slave,

creator and monster—it is our sworn fate to

find duality in an ever-disintegrating universe

where we are ourselves the destroying angel.

Ours is not to simply imagine into existence

our deepest fears, but to learn how to vanquish

our desire to stand still as we sink into death—

make our way to the other side, where we

might find a renaissance of the will and spirit;

perhaps another reason with each new breath.

We are only human, after all, and we can only

move as fast as our hearts will permit, find only

that which our hearts desire. We must each

set the bar each morning as we greet the new day,

as each new day is certain to find us, willing or not.

Letter to Evans in January

Dear friend, I'm hunting hope
the way you search for keys
you just had in your hand.
I wake up early & walk a mile.
I try to recall my dreams, hazy
narratives of a beach town
I've never seen. Real cold never
comes until the first of the year.
Spring's still months away.
Why is January a resolution
& a promise to get our lives right?
Hot weather melts the secrets
alive in our pores. The cruelest month?
July in South Georgia, the heat
like the devil's breath, a bad bourbon
burn. Then, I wish for winter.
Days lean into days until the months
collapse into gray memory.
I hang onto small things—my wife's
palms, the gap in my daughter's teeth,
my son's habit of walking on tiptoes.
I understand. In this new year,

everything groans like rotted wood.
I worry I'll fall through the floor.
Hold on tight as the walls press in,
my friend. Houses always collapse.

Letter to Newberry: January 31, 2017

Dear Jeff: This morning a fog
rests on the valley
like a weary traveler, looking
for comfort. Normally I can see
across the entire basin
as the sun rises far to the east
even in the Winter months,
but today I can see only half
a mile at most. The white dissolve
of cold air trapped beneath
a warm cushion has left
hoarfrost on the dormant roses
and spreads like spider silk on
all of the car windshields lining
the streets. Counting songbirds
I have witnessed over thirty species
of wild animals passing through
this small town. Last night
towards dusk, a Western Screech Owl
perched in our Spanish Olive Tree
before taking flight in a wide arc
past our window then over

the tops of our neighbors' houses,
feathers stretched out like fingers
pointing to the distant horizon
of this wide desert bowl, lined with
ancient sandstone formations.
The new year has turned for us
and the future lies beyond
those weather torn hills, and though
I know it's time to pick up and walk,
part of me knows I will be forced to
navigate by instinct until the haze
burns away. All the best, Justin

Letter to Evans Instead of a Postscript

Justin, when you unseal this poem, remember
that it is made of voice the way that music is made
from the guitar player's deft fingers,
from the pianist's slow arpeggios.
Ever hear your own voice on tape, recorded?
You sound different, older sometimes. I hear
my ragged breath, the constant half-laughs,
as though I'm one snort away from guffaw.
You know that's not true—I'm brimmed
with sadness most days. I see not pine trees
or fields of ripe cantaloupes. I see rotting
vegetation. I see strip-cut forests.
So that voice is a kind of lie, yes, even
recorded? If you're looking for truth,
take a liar with you. No one ever said
that to me, but it sounds good, looks good
written here. Hear this, man: I'm a liar.
So are you. My students think poems are diaries,
but mere records of life fall into banal
observation. I stayed on Lake Blackshear
a few years ago & journaled each morning.
I wrote about the sound of morning birds,

the wind off the lake, the humming buzz
of carpenter bees. I wrote about Jake York's
death, a wound still gaping, then, a hole
left. He was *il miglior fabbro*, the Southern son
of a Southern son who told me once that he
wasn't trying to save the world. He just wanted
to write poems that needed to be written.
I think that's the same thing. His poems
were not records of what was, but tributes
to what should be. Isn't that the whole of it?
Let's call it jazz. Let's call it *duende*.
Let's call it another image of my father
echoing, reverberating in my mind: the old man
lighting a cigarette, taking up a guitar,
& singing the same song one more time.
             Join me in the chorus, Jeff.

Letter to Newberry: Coda

Jeff: It is foolish for anyone to think
they can un-see what has been seen,
but I know I have un-learned many
lessons my grandfather taught me, or,
if I am going to take responsibility,
what he tried to teach me, the failure
belonging only to myself. I would
like to think my poems are how things
really happened, not just how I wanted
them to be. Perhaps that is why
I write my poems in the first place.
I am trying to re-write the past, perform
my best magic trick in making people
believe my version of events is gospel.
You'll never make a living writing
your poems, I keep repeating over in
my head, though I know nobody ever
once told me that. But my grandmother,
when I was about seventeen, did tell me
my desire to write poems would pass
like a storm in the night leaving only
the slightest hint it was ever there. Still,

there are so many times when one thing
is said but I hear something else.
Where do I begin to revise the past I have
already revised? When is it required I
own up to all of the lies I have told?
Who will be my confessor? There is
the parable of the boy who cried wolf,
his cautionary tale comes to mind, and I
think it applies to us in part. When we lie,
we are asking for an audience just like
the boy, and once we have one, we are
never sure what to do with the people
who have appeared. Maybe that's what
happened to poetry. Maybe we promised
something miraculous one time too many
and the world has wizened up since then.

About the Correspondents

Jeff Newberry was born on the Florida Gulf Coast and returns there any time he gets a free moment. He teaches composition, creative writing, and literature at Abraham Baldwin Agricultural College in South Georgia, where he lives with his wife, his son, and his daughter, who was born with Spina Bifida. His books include the novel *A Stairway to the Sea* (Pulpwood Press, 2016) and *Brackish* (Aldrich Press, 2012). With the poet Brent House, he is the co-editor of *The Gulf Stream: Poems of the Gulf Coast* (Snake Nation Press, 2013). Find him online at www.jeffnewberry.com.

Justin Evans was born and raised in Utah. After graduating from high school, Justin served in the U.S. Army and then attended college in Utah. Later, he graduated with a Master's Degree from the University of Nevada, Reno. His books include *Town for the Trees* (Foothills Publishing, 2011), *Hobble Creek Almanac* (Aldrich Press, 2013), and *Sailing This Nameless Ship* (BlazeVOX, 2013). He lives in rural Nevada with his wife and sons, where he teaches at the local high school.

59660726R00067

Made in the USA
Columbia, SC
07 June 2019